THE LITTLE PUPFISH
OF SALT CREEK

Written and Illustrated
by

Patricia S. Brandt

ABOUT THE AUTHOR

Patricia S. Brandt taught life science and physical science for seventeen years in grades ranging from elementary and junior high to high school and college. She also created and implemented a wide variety of nature programs and lessons designed for an outdoor environment. She holds a B.S. Ed. degree from Southwest Missouri State University, an M. Ed. degree from Drury College, and Rank I certification from Eastern Kentucky University.

Her appreciation and understanding of nature, combined with her concern for children, prompted the author to create this book. It is the author's hope that her work will help children to understand, respect, and protect their natural world.

ISBN 0-9649493-0-X

I bet you never thought about fish living in the desert! That's right, some fish do live in the desert and they have for thousands of years! As you read and color the pictures in this book, you will be learning about the Salt Creek Pupfish. It is only one of the five kinds of pupfish that live in Death Valley National Park.

This little fish is less than two (2") inches long. The ONLY place on earth where this pupfish is found is in Salt Creek, located in Death Valley National Park. The water in Salt Creek flows out of a spring.

The water in the spring comes from water moving under the ground from another area of the park. This water is very salty, more than twice as salty as the water in the ocean. Even the air smells salty, like the air you breath when you visit an ocean beach!

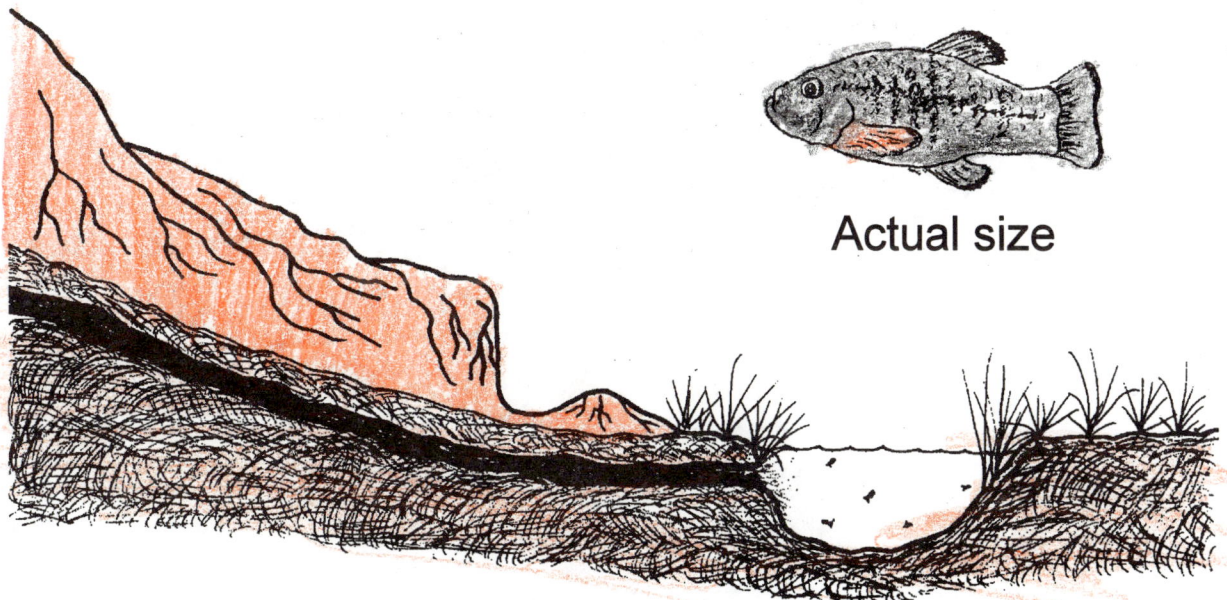

Actual size

Several little channels of water from Salt Creek weave back and forth in all different directions as Salt Creek flows away from the spring. You cannot see the spring from the parking lot or hiking trail because it is two miles up the canyon.

If you could fly like a bird, this is what you would see from the air as you flew above Salt Creek.

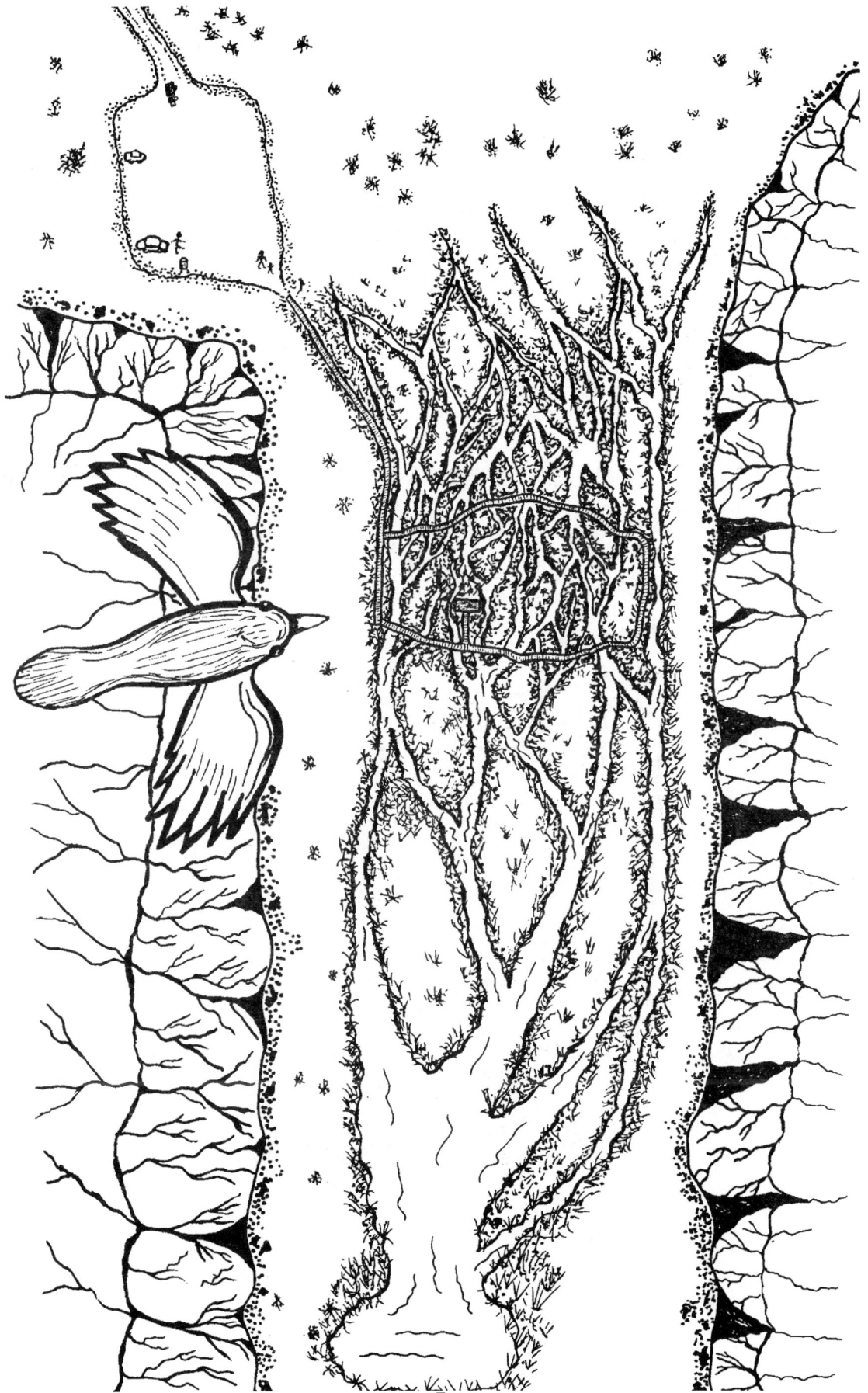

Death Valley is the hottest and driest place in North America. Temperatures during the summer can be over 120°F and less than 2" of rain falls there a year. It is hard to believe that a little fish can live in this desert, but it does!

How hot does it get where you live and how much rain do you get during one year?

The map on the next page will help you find the home of the Salt Creek Pupfish.

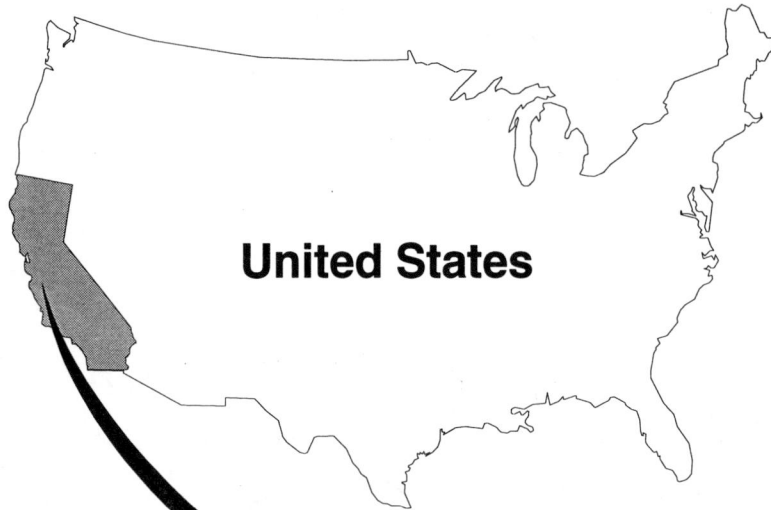

United States

The State of California

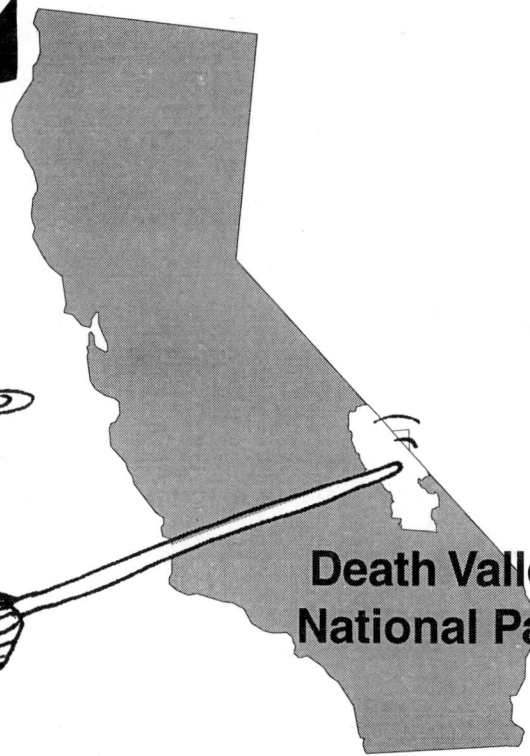

Death Valley
National Park

People from all over the world come to the United States to visit Death Valley National Park. In fact, more than one million (l,000,000) people visit the park every year!

Because so many of these visitors go to Salt Creek to see the little pupfish, the park rangers had to build a path made out of wood. This path is called a boardwalk and it helps to protect the plants and animals from the many people that visit and walk all over this area.

Even though there is now a boardwalk, people still have to be careful they do not step on little animals like this little horned lizard that might crawl up on the trail to sun itself!

It is very important not to harm any of the plants or animals at Salt Creek or anywhere else in the park. You also need to remember to leave rocks, flowers, and even arrowheads in any park where you find them. Did you know that it is even against the law to harm or take anything from a National Park? Now you do and I bet you can guess why?

If you think it is because the parks are for everyone to enjoy, and the animals and plants should be respected, you are on the right "boardwalk!"

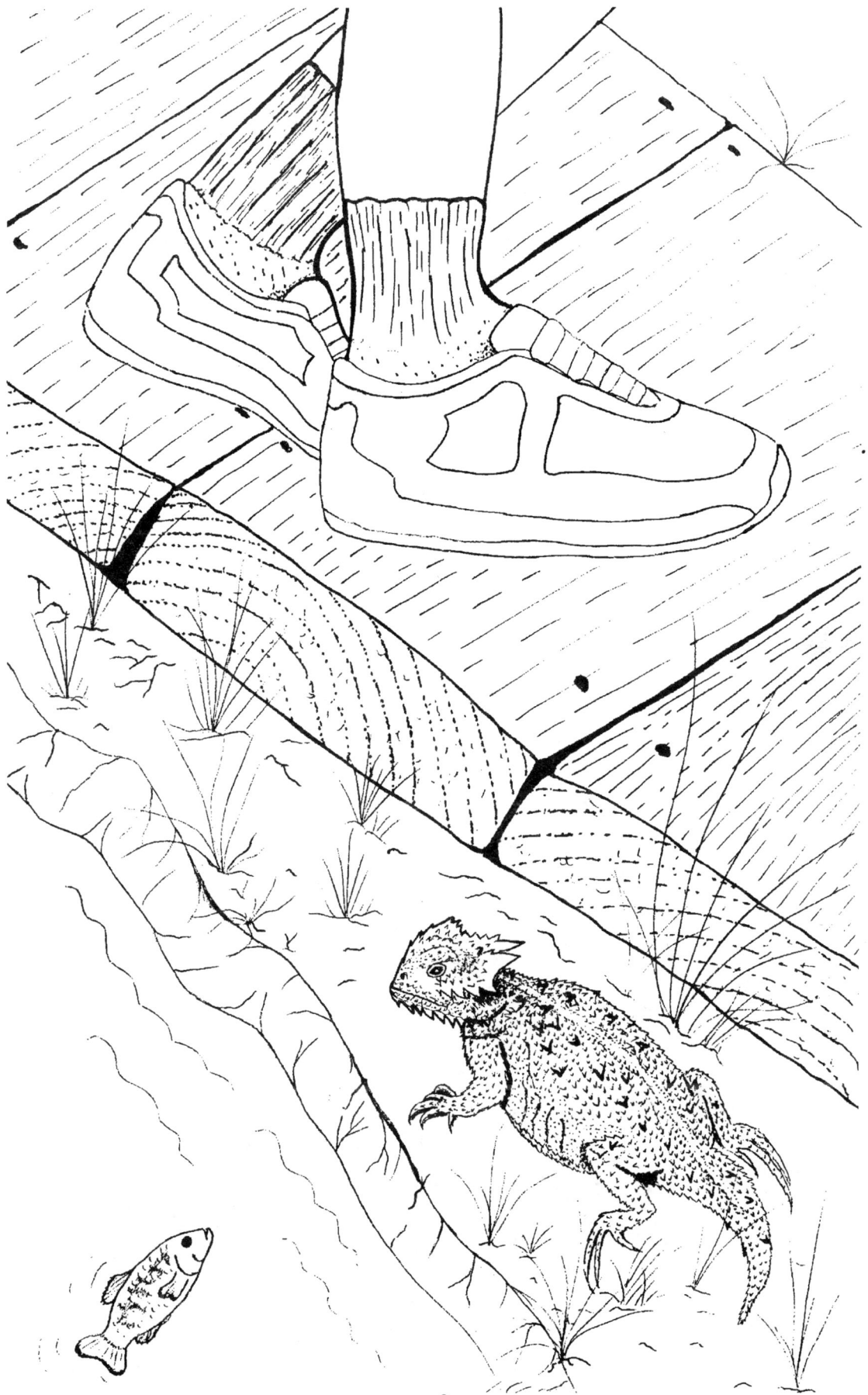

The boardwalk helps protect people too! They don't have to worry about getting wet or stuck in the mud or walking through loose, sandy soil.

Maybe you should draw two more children in this picture. Do you think they remembered to take water, sun screen, and a hat? You better draw that in too! It can get very hot in Death Valley!

It is easy to find your way around Salt Creek, all you have to do is follow the one-half (l/2) mile wooden boardwalk.   The boardwalk takes you over bridges and along the edge of the flowing water of Salt Creek.

If you look very carefully, you might see one of the little pupfish darting back and forth in the shallow water.

If you visit Salt Creek in the Spring, you will have the best chance to find hundreds of little fish moving rapidly through the water. Schools of fish scurry away as you look down at them from the boardwalk. They know you are there because of your shadow and your movements.

14

The pupfish dart in one direction and then in another as you watch them. Faster and faster they swim until they reach a very shallow area where the water is less than one (1") inch deep. This will not stop them, they will just wiggle over the rocks and go into deeper water!

Not all kinds of fish can do that!

It is fun to stand very still and watch the pupfish. Within a few weeks, the heat of the summer sun will dry up much of their watery world. Only a few will survive the hot summer by living in deeper pools of water located near the spring.

The pupfish who live through the summer and cold winter will produce more fish next spring when the waters will again flow in Salt Creek. It is important for many little fish to hatch each spring in order to replace the large number of fish that die during the hot summer. This is how the pupfish have survived for thousands of years!

Look, here is a male pupfish! He has been chasing other males away from his territory while he waits for a brown colored female pupfish to come by and deposit her eggs. The female is a little smaller than the male.

When you color him, remember that he has blue and purple breeding colors on his body scales, his tail fin has a black tip and he has black colored stripes on his sides.

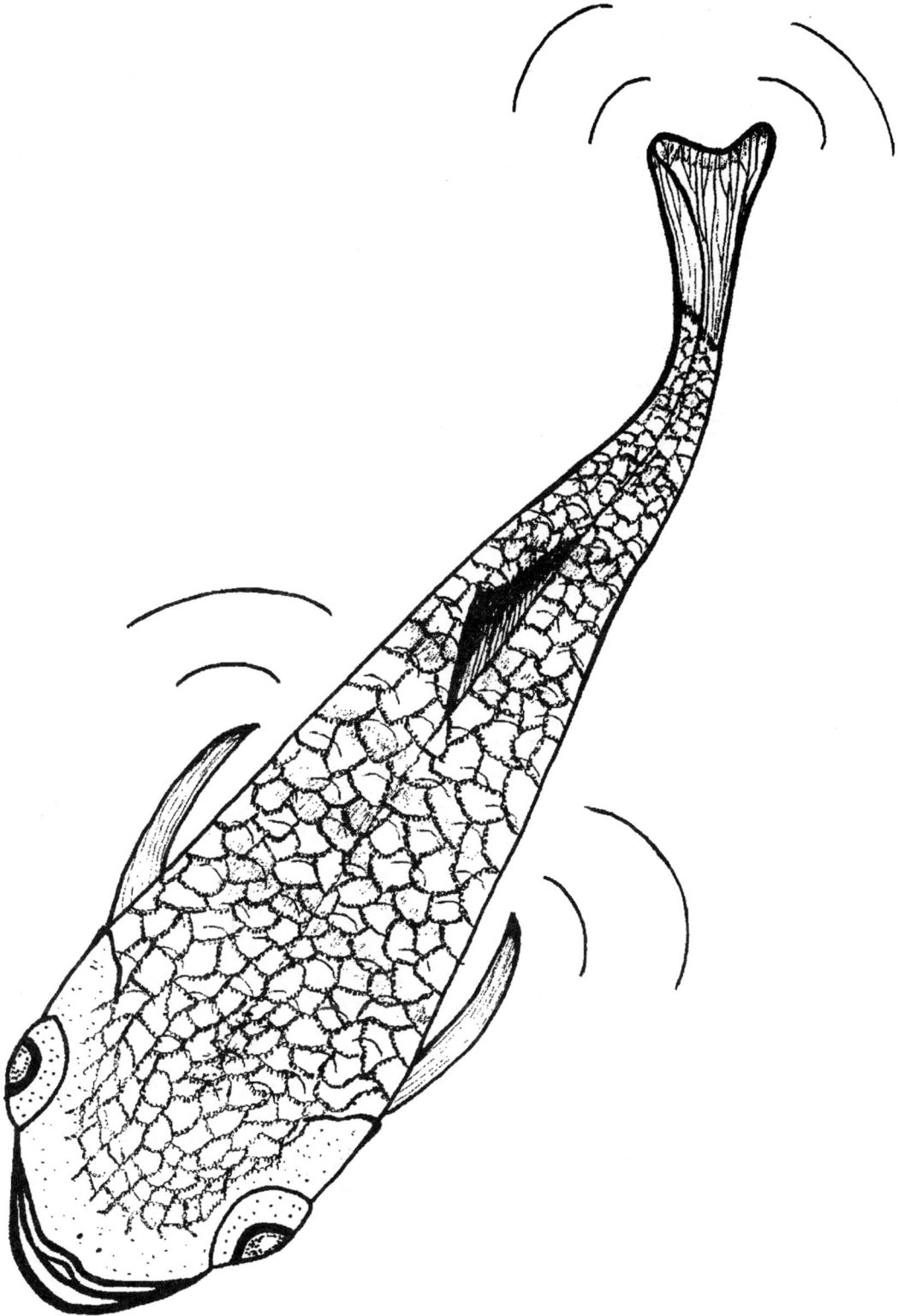

If you live in a place that gets cold during the winter, what do you do when you want to go outside? You probably put on a coat!

The little pupfish does not have a coat, but it does have mud! That's right, mud!

The little fish digs down in the mud during the cold winter days. Scientists studying the pupfish have even found them down in the mud under the water when it is very hot. Why do you think they might go down in the mud during part of the summer?

You are right if you said they might need to cool off!
Remember, Death Valley can get <u>very</u> hot in the summer.

The pupfish eat a small greenish-brown plant called algae that floats on the surface or settles on the bottom of the water. The algae makes up most of their diet, but they also eat small insects living in the water and insects that fall into the water from the air. They have even been known to eat the dead bodies of other pupfish.

The pupfish are a very important part of the food chain in the Salt Creek area. They eat the small plants and animals in their watery world and the larger animals eat them. Birds, such as ravens, egrets and great blue herons, keep a constant lookout along the shore for a tasty pupfish.

This tiny fish is hiding in the shadow of the pickleweed plant. The pickleweed is found all over the Salt Creek area. It grows very well in the wet, salty soil that is found here. The green branches look like rows of little green pickles hooked together on a string!

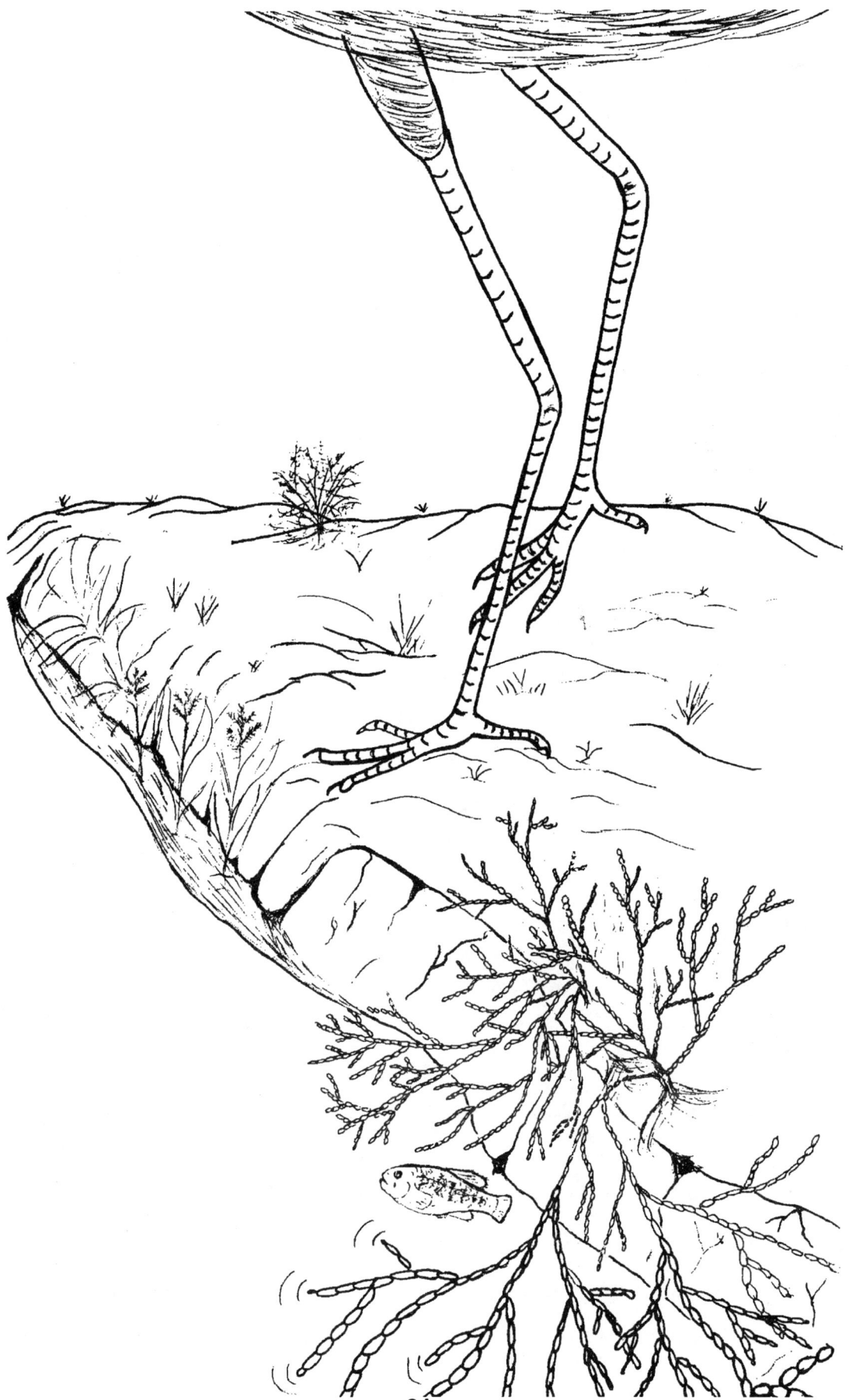

When the coyote visits Salt Creek, the little pupfish
see movement and hide. These two are hiding in the
shadow of the salt grass.

If you look very carefully, you might find some animal
tracks in this area. Most of the animals here are active at

night when it is cool. Only their tracks let you know they were there at all. The coyote tracks look like those of a domestic dog.

Don't forget to look in the mud in the shallow water of the creek! You might just find some animal tracks like the ones this little pupfish has discovered from the coyote.

Many lizards, mice and beetles live here among the plants. See if you can find their tracks in the sandy soil by the side of the boardwalk.

Here are some hints to tell each one from the other:

- the lizard drags its tail between its feet

- the beetle leaves a track like a little railroad

- the mice leave prints that look like little hands

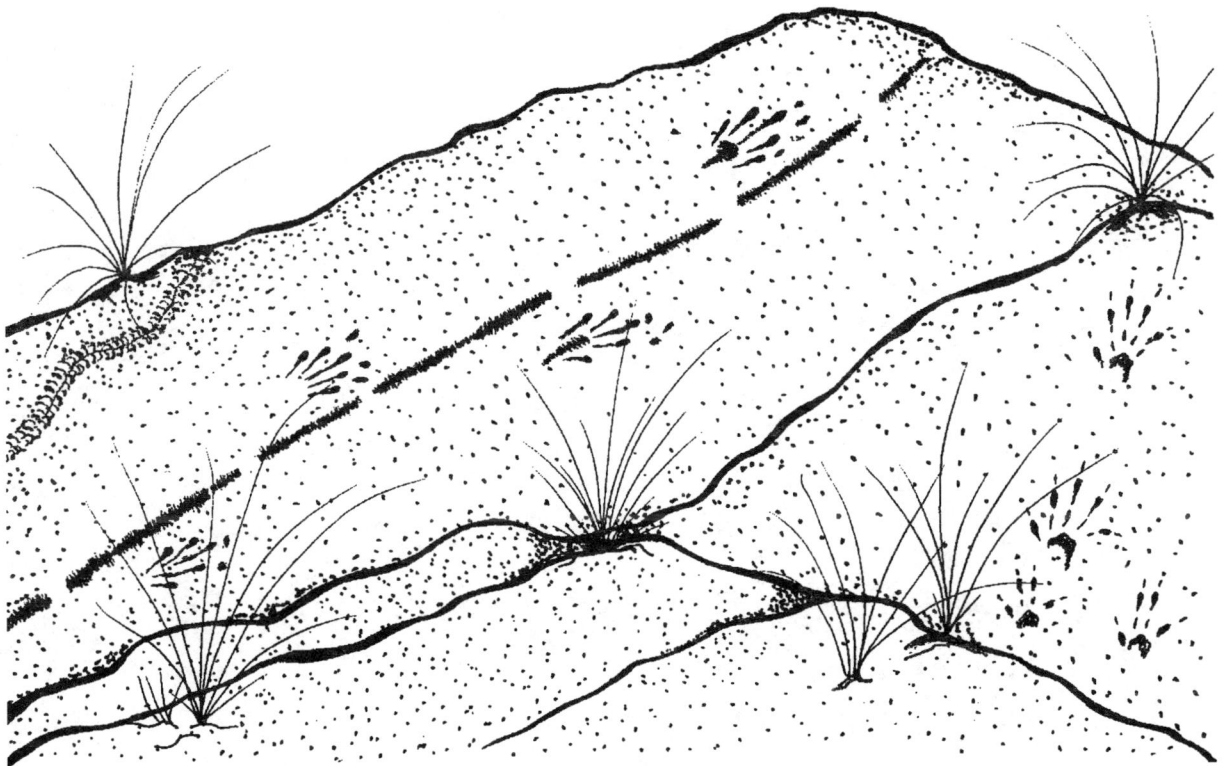

Animals are not the only ones that like to eat the pupfish. Many years ago the Native American Indians of this area used baskets to catch the tiny pupfish.

The baskets were made out of plants collected and woven together by the Indians. The little fish were caught by the thousands during the spring, then they were baked and eaten.

The Indians had to eat many different kinds of food in order to survive. The pupfish were a good source of protein.

If you look very carefully into still pools of water, you might see aquatic insects swimming around or crawling on the bottom.

Look for small, brown beetles that are about the size of a sunflower seed. When you find them, watch how they kick their little legs to move through the water. They are very active. They move up and down and sometimes they even dig down into the bottom of the creek bed!

Actual size

29

Another aquatic insect found in Salt Creek is the water boatmen. They move their legs rapidly when disturbed. Their jerking motions give them away as they propel themselves through the water.

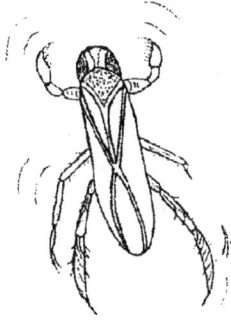

Actual Size

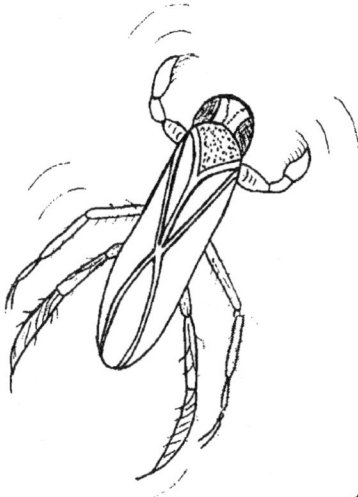

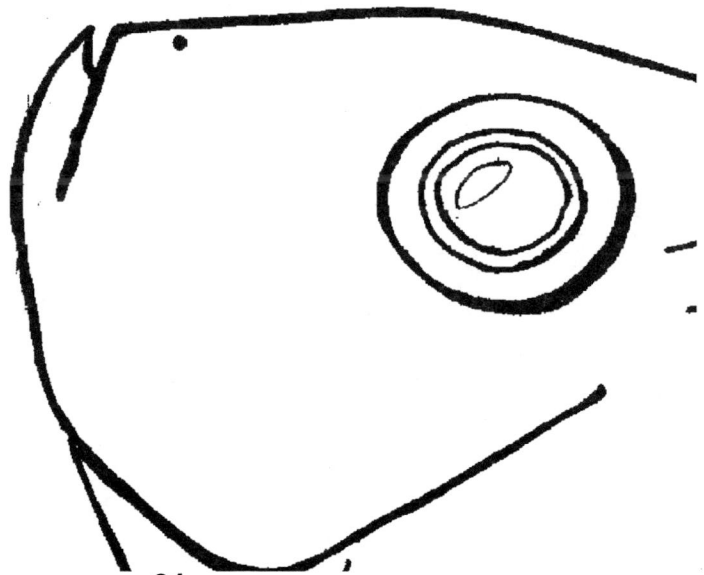

31

Horse flies, caddisflies, and dragonflies can be seen flying over the Salt Creek area.   These insects spend the early part of their life cycle in the water before becoming adults. Now they fly above the water and sometimes land on a plant to rest.

Huge horse flies like this one can bite people, so keep an eye out for them!

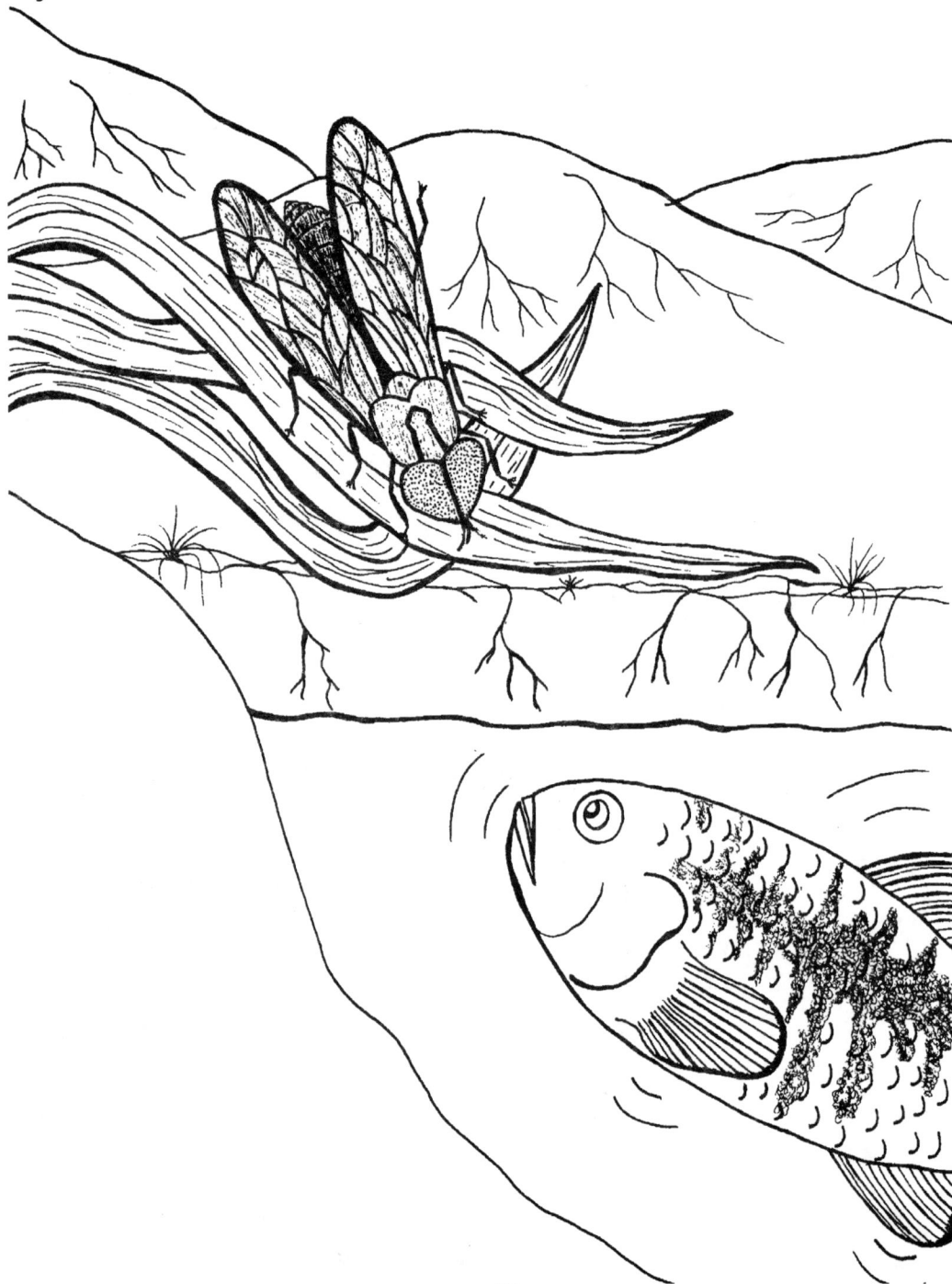

This caddisfly and pupfish are looking each other over very carefully. The caddisfly is free to fly away, but the pupfish must remain behind as the heat of the summer sun dries out much of its watery world.

What a dangerous place for the little pupfish to live!

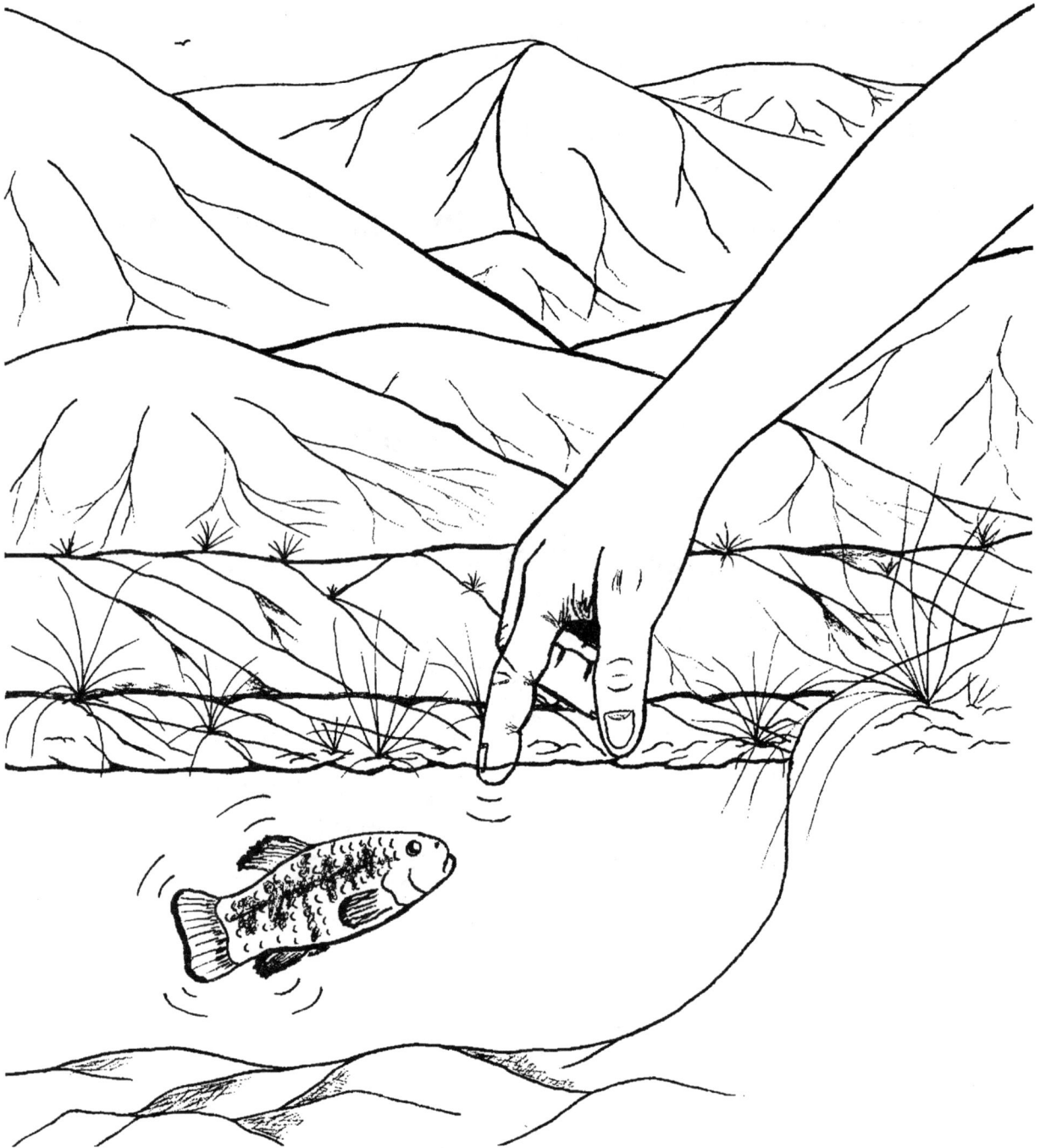

If you stick your finger in the water, it will probably feel warm. Not only do the pupfish live in a desert, they live in warm, salty water in the desert! But the water of Death Valley has not always been this way!

Over ten thousand (10,000) years ago Death Valley was covered by deep, fresh water lakes. The fish living in these lakes could swim freely for hundreds of miles. The large lakes dried up and many of the fish died. Only one type of fish was able to survive and adapt as this world of water dried up around them. These fish were the ancestors of the little pupfish in this story

Today, each type of pupfish has a small, watery world of its own where it lives in harmony with its surroundings. When people visit Death Valley National Park, they need to remember to **leave the little fish where they are** so that nature can control the numbers of fish that live, reproduce and even die each year.

If you have enjoyed learning about the Salt Creek Pupfish, you might want to find out more about the other animals and plants found in Death Valley National Park, the hottest and driest place in North America. Just think, if fish can live there, so can many other strange and interesting forms of life! See what you can discover about the other animals and plants that DARE to call Death Valley home!

THE END OF THIS TAIL!

MORE INTERESTING INFORMATION ABOUT PUPFISH

A pupfish usually lives 3 to 6 months and it is very rare to find one living to be older than 2 or 3 years.

When pupfish are 3 months old, they can spawn and reproduce more pupfish.

The scientific name for the Salt Creek Pupfish is *Cyprinodon salinus salinus.*

LISTED BELOW ARE THE COMMON NAMES, SCIENTIFIC NAMES AND THE LOCATIONS WHERE FOUR OTHER TYPES OF PUPFISH CAN BE FOUND LIVING.

1.) The Amargosa Pupfish (*Cyprinodon nevadensis amargosae*), is found in the Amargosa River, northwest of Saratoga Springs.

2.) The Saratoga Pupfish (*Cyprinodon nevadensis nevadensis*), is found in Saratoga Springs at the south end of Death Valley National Park.

3.) The Devils Hole Pupfish (*Cyprinodon diabolis*), is found in Devils Hole in western Nevada, a short distance east of Death Valley National Park.

4.) The Cottonball Marsh Pupfish (*Cyprinodon salinus milleri*), is found in Cottonball Marsh located five miles south of Salt Creek.

This book is dedicated:

To all who love to explore the outdoors and who respect nature.

To all of the devoted students I taught for seventeen years.

To my parents and sisters for all they have taught me.

My Mother for teaching me kindness and to be excited by the world around me.

My Father for teaching me perseverance and determination.

My sister, Anna, for her love of plants and her gentle nature.

My sister, Marjie, for her love and devotion to family.

My sister, Nancy, for her strength to overcome any loss and to adapt to change.

AND

To my husband for his belief in my abilities.